When Marian Sang

The True Recital of Marian Anderson

The Voice of a Century

Libretto by...........PAM MUÑOZ RYAN

Staging by..............BRIAN SELZNICK

HAMPTON-BROWN

THE EXCHANGE

How can the actions of one person affect the next generation?

It was her range of notes

that caused all the commotion.

With one breath she sounded like rain,

sprinkling high notes in the morning sun.

And with the next she was thunder,

resounding deep in a dark sky.

Dedicated to the memory of Richard Selznick whose recollections inspired this book.

When Marian Sang by Pam Muñoz Ryan, pictures by Brian Selznick. Published by Scholastic Press, a division of Scholastic, Inc. Text copyright © 2002 by Pam Muñoz Ryan. Illustrations copyright © 2002 by Brian Selznick. Cover illustrations © 2002 by Brian Selznick. All rights reserved. Reprinted by permission of Scholastic, Inc.

On-Page Coach ™ (introductions, questions, on-page glossaries), The Exchange, back cover summary © Hampton-Brown.

Hampton-Brown
P.O. Box 223220
Carmel, California 93922
800-333-3510
www.hampton-brown.com

Printed in the United States of America

ISBN-13: 978-0-7362-2781-0
ISBN-10: 0-7362-2781-4

07 08 09 10 11 12 13 14 10 9 8 7 6 5 4

Marian loves to sing. She performs at churches when she is only eight years old. She applies to a music school, but they will not accept her. Why? Because she is African American.

No one was surprised

that Marian loved to sing. **After all**, she listened to Father singing in the morning as he dressed. Mother often hummed while she worked in the kitchen. Sometimes Marian and her little sisters, Ethel May and Alyse, sang songs all afternoon.

Let us break bread together
*   on our knees*
Let us break bread together
*   on our knees*
When I fall on my knees
*   with my face to the rising sun*
O Lord, have mercy on me.

However, *her* voice was **distinct**—strong and **velvety** and able to **climb more than twenty-four notes**.

Everyone wanted to hear Marian sing.

....

After all Especially since

distinct special

velvety smooth, comforting

climb more than twenty-four notes sing high and low notes

Alexander Robinson, the choir director at the Union Baptist Church in South Philadelphia, wanted to hear Marian sing even though she was not quite eight years old and sometimes sang *too* loud. He asked her to **perform a duet** with her friend Viola Johnson. As Viola sang the high part and Marian sang the low, their harmony blended like a silk braid.

Dear to the heart of the Shepherd
Dear are the sheep of His fold
Dear is the love that He gives them
Dearer than silver or gold.

Church folks started whispering and **followed with out-and-out talking** about Marian's remarkable gift.

Neighboring churches heard the news and invited Marian to perform. One advertisement said: "COME AND HEAR THE BABY CONTRALTO, TEN YEARS OLD." And people came.

---

perform a duet sing a song

followed with out-and-out talking then talking to other people

Neighboring churches heard the news People who went to churches nearby learned about Marian's voice

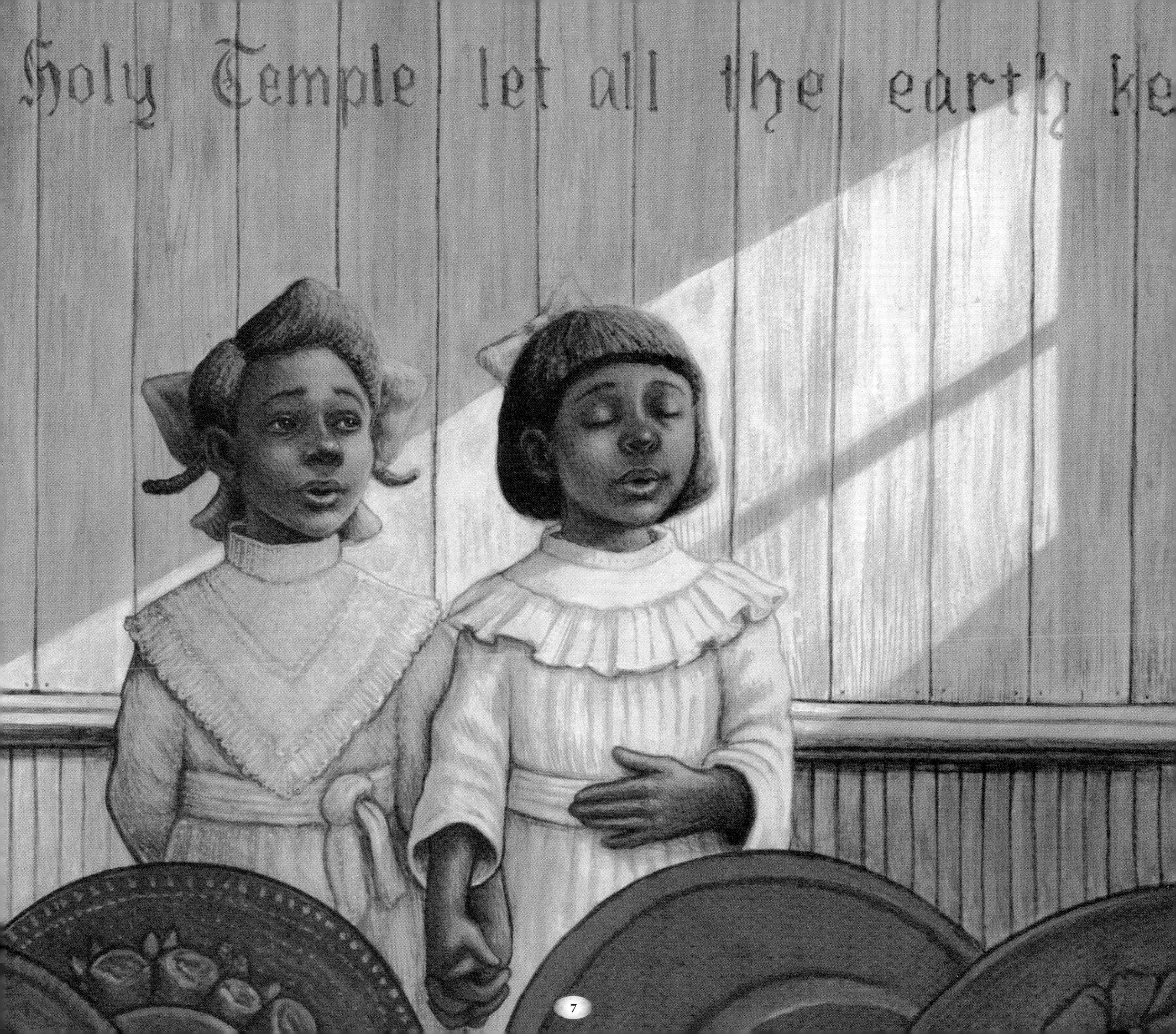
Holy Temple let all the earth ke

When Marian sang, it was often with her eyes closed, as if finding the music within. Audiences heard not only words, but feelings, too: spirited worship, tender affection, and **nothing short of joy**.

She was chosen for the celebrated People's Chorus, a hundred voices from all the black church **choirs** in Philadelphia. She was one of the youngest members and had to stand on a chair so those in back could see the pride of South Philadelphia.

Her father was proud, too, but protective. He didn't want anyone **taking advantage of** his child. Father's love made Marian feel important. When he died after an injury at the Reading Terminal where he sold ice, **tragedy** filled Marian's heart and sometimes her songs.

Were you there when they laid Him
in the tomb?
Were you there when they laid Him
in the tomb?
Oh . . . oh . . . sometimes it causes me
to tremble, tremble, tremble
Were you there when they laid Him
in the tomb?

....

nothing short of joy happiness

choirs singing groups

taking advantage of hurting, using

tragedy sadness

BEFORE YOU MOVE ON...

1. **Text Feature** Why do some words on pages 4, 6, and 8 look different from the rest of the words?

2. **Inference** Reread page 8. Why did Marian's father think that people would try to take advantage of Marian?

LOOK AHEAD Read pages 10–13 to see what happens when Marian tries to go to music school.

Mother was happy for Marian's success but reminded her that no matter what she studied to **take a little extra time** and do it well.

Marian didn't need extra encouragement when it came to singing. She practiced her part of each song and often learned all the other parts, too. For her, music was **serious business**, and more than anything, she hoped to someday go to music school. Church members **promised tuition** for "our Marian" if she was accepted.

---

take a little extra time work hard

serious business very important

promised tuition said that they would pay the school fees

Since Father's death, Marian worked at **odd** jobs and sang in concert programs in order to help **support** her family. It wasn't until 1915, when Marian was eighteen, that she finally went to a music school and patiently waited in line for an application. But the girl behind the counter helped everyone except Marian. **Was she invisible?**

Finally, the girl said, "We don't take **colored**!" Her voice sounded like a steel door clanking shut.

---

odd different

support pay for food and other needs for

Was she invisible? Couldn't the girl see her?

colored African Americans

Marian knew about **prejudice**. She had seen the **trolley** drive past her family as they stood at the corner. She knew that her people were always the last to be helped in a store. But she could not understand how anyone who was surrounded by the spirit and beauty of music could be so **narrow-minded**.

She felt sick in her stomach and in her heart. Didn't they know that her skin was different but her feelings were the same? Couldn't she be a professional singer if she was **a Negro**?

With **unwavering faith**, Mother told her that there would be another way to accomplish what would have been done at that school. Marian believed her mother. She took voice lessons in her own neighborhood, continued with the choirs, and sometimes performed at Negro churches and colleges.

....

prejudice people who thought they were better than others; people who judged others by their race

trolley bus

narrow-minded unaccepting

a Negro an African American

unwavering faith certainty

BEFORE YOU MOVE ON...

1. **Details** The music school would not accept Marian. Why was life challenging for Marian when she was a child?

2. **Summarize** Reread pages 10–11. What kind of person was Marian?

LOOK AHEAD Read pages 14–19 to see if Marian will take voice lessons from a famous teacher.

*Marian performs in many places.
She dreams of being an opera singer. She learns
from a famous musician. Then, she travels to
Europe to perform.*

When Marian saw a Metropolitan Opera performance of the **tragic** opera *Madame Butterfly*, **thoughts of a formal music education again came to mind**. How wonderful it would be to sing on a grand stage, **act out a dramatic role**, and wear beautiful costumes. The **passionate music inspired her** and she was determined to study. But opera was simply the sun and the moon—a dream that seemed too far away to reach.

> *He's got the wind and the rain*
> *in His hands*
> *He's got the sun and the moon*
> *right in His hands*
> *He's got the wind and the rain*
> *in His hands*
> *He's got the whole world in His hands.*

....

tragic very sad

thoughts of a formal music education again came to mind Marian thought again about going to music school

act out a dramatic role play a character

passionate music inspired her beautiful music made her want to succeed

15

As a young woman in her twenties, Marian was invited to many states to sing. Sometimes she traveled with her **accompanist** by train where they were seated in the dirty and crowded **Jim Crow car reserved for Negroes**. When she arrived at her destination, she often sang the same program twice, to separate audiences—one white and one black—or to segregated groups, whites in the best seats and blacks in the balcony. Many times, she was welcomed enthusiastically by her audiences, and then could not get a hotel room because she was Negro.

No matter **what humiliations she endured**, Marian **sang her heart with dignity**. Her voice left audiences weeping or in hushed awe as they strained to hold on to the memory of every **opulent note**.

When Israel was in Egypt's Land
Let my people go
Oppressed so hard they could not stand
Let my people go
Go down Moses
Way down in Egypt's Land
Tell ol' Pharaoh
To let my people go.

---

accompanist piano player

Jim Crow car reserved for Negroes train car where African Americans had to sit

what humiliations she endured how she was treated

sang her heart with dignity sang beautifully

opulent note beautiful word she sang

Marian still wanted to **advance her singing with master teachers**. With the help of friends, she was **granted an audition with** the fierce yet famous Giuseppe Boghetti.

When she arrived at his studio, Mr. Boghetti announced that he didn't have time or room for new students. Too afraid even to look at him, Marian took a deep breath. Slowly, with great emotion, she sang,

> *"Deep river, my home is over Jordan*
> *Deep river, Lord, I want to cross over*
> > *into campground*
> *Don't you want to go to that gospel feast*
> *That promised land where all is peace?*
> *O, deep river, Lord, I want to cross over*
> > *into campground."*

Marian finally **lifted her eyes**.

"I will **make room for** you right away," Mr. Boghetti said firmly, "and I will need only two years with you. After that, you will be able to go anywhere and sing for anybody."

Again, Marian's devoted church community raised the money for her lessons.

---

advance her singing with master teachers become a better singer by studying with the best teachers

granted an audition with given a chance to sing for

lifted her eyes looked at Mr. Boghetti

make room for start teaching

BEFORE YOU MOVE ON...

1. **Conclusions** Reread page 19. Mr. Boghetti said he would not take new students, but then he changed his mind. Why?

2. **Paraphrase** Reread page 15. What does it mean that "opera was simply the sun and the moon—a dream that seemed too far away to reach"?

LOOK AHEAD Read pages 20–23 to see where Marian travels.

ILE DE FRANCE

Marian worked hard with Mr. Boghetti, and sometimes, for practice, she sang scenes from Italian operas with him. Her **recitals** now included German songs, too, but other languages troubled her. She didn't want simply to sing beautiful words like *Dunkel, wie dunkel in Wald und in Feld!* She wanted to know that the words meant *Dark, how dark in the woods and the fields!*

Other Negro singers had gone overseas to develop their voices and learn foreign languages. Why not her? After all, Europe was different. There, she would be able to sing to **mixed audiences** and travel without the restrictions put on her people in America.

Marian needed to **grow** and Mother agreed.

A bundle of trepidation and excitement, Marian boarded the *Ile de France* in October 1927. She had never been so far from her family. She knew her sisters would take good care of Mother, but still she already felt twinges of homesickness.

---

recitals shows, performances

mixed audiences audiences with people of different cultures

grow learn and experience more

A bundle of trepidation and excitement Feeling nervous and excited

Sometimes I feel like a motherless child

Sometimes I feel like a motherless child

Sometimes I feel like a motherless child

A long ways from home. A long ways from home.

Sometimes I feel like I'm almost gone

Sometimes I feel like I'm almost gone

Sometimes I feel like I'm almost gone

A long ways from home. A long ways from home.

BEFORE YOU MOVE ON...

1. **Main Idea and Details** Why was the trip to Europe important for Marian?

2. **Author's Purpose** Look at the song on pages 22–23. Why did the author put it here?

LOOK AHEAD Read pages 24–29 to find out why Marian cannot perform in the United States.

Marian returns to the United States. But many concert halls will not allow her to perform. Though she struggles, in the end, her dreams come true.

Marian studied and was eventually invited to perform in concert halls in Norway, Sweden, Finland, and Denmark. **The enthusiasm for her singing was so overwhelming** that one newspaper in Sweden called it "Marian Fever."

Audiences applauded in London, cheered in Paris, and pounded on the stage for **encores** in Russia. In Austria, the world-famous conductor, Arturo Toscanini, announced that what he had heard, one was **privileged** to hear only once in a hundred years.

The enthusiasm for her singing was so overwhelming
So many people liked Marian's singing

encores Marian to sing again
privileged lucky

Marian felt as if she had finally achieved some success. She even asked Mother if there was anything she wanted that would make her happy because now Marian **could afford** to buy it for her. Mother said that all she wanted was for God to

hold Marian in the highest of His hands.

It seemed like **she was already there**.

Mr. Boghetti had been right. She *could* go anywhere and sing for anyone . . .

....

could afford had money

....

hold Marian in the highest of His hands love and protect Marian

she was already there that was already happening

. . . until she came home to the United States.

In 1939, Howard University in Washington, D.C., **booked** a concert with Marian Anderson and began looking for an auditorium big enough to **hold the audience she attracted**. They decided that the 4,000-seat Constitution Hall would be perfect. But the manager of the hall said it wasn't available *and* no other dates were offered because of their *white performers only* **policy**.

Marian's agent, Sol Hurok, wrote to the hall manager, **pointing out** that Marian Anderson was one of the greatest living singers of our time. But it did no good.

---

booked set up; scheduled

hold the audience she attracted fit all of the people who would come to see Marian

policy rule

pointing out saying

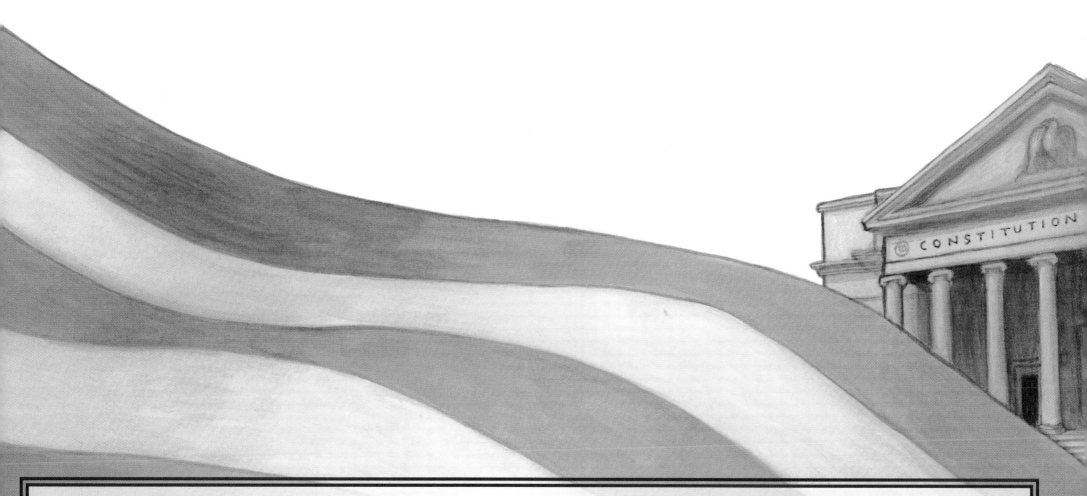

Enraged fans wrote letters to the newspaper. In protest, Eleanor Roosevelt, the first lady of the United States, **resigned from the organization that sponsored** Constitution Hall.

Howard University then tried to **reserve** a large high school auditorium from an all-white school. Again, they were **denied**. Now teachers were angry and marched in support of Marian in front of the Board of Education. **Washington, D.C., was a boiling pot about to spill over.**

Wasn't there someplace in her own country's capital where Marian Anderson's voice could be heard?

Enraged Angry

resigned from the organization that sponsored said that she would not be a part of the group that paid for

reserve use

---

denied told no

Washington, D.C., was a boiling pot about to spill over. People in Washington, D.C., were very angry.

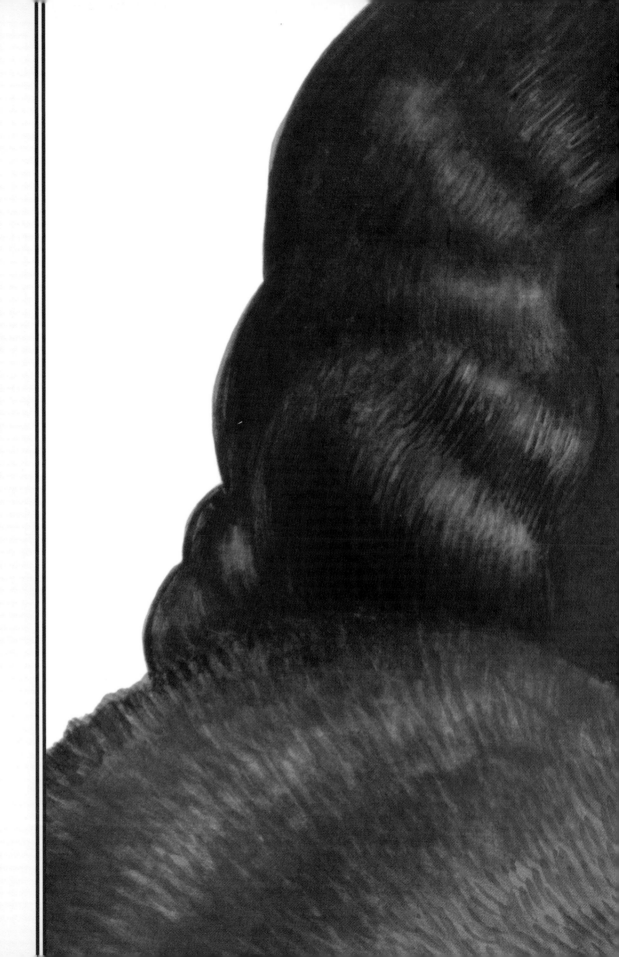

Committees formed and held meetings.
Finally, with President Roosevelt's approval, the
Department of the Interior of the United States
government invited Marian to sing on the steps
of the Lincoln Memorial on Easter Sunday. Her
country was offering her **a momentous** invitation,
but she **had concerns**. Would people protest? Was it
dangerous? Would anyone come?

Examining her heart, Marian realized that
although she was a singer first and foremost, she
also had become a symbol to her people and she
wanted to make it easier for those who would
follow her.

She said yes.

Standing in the shadow of the statue of Lincoln,
waiting to be called out, she read the engraved
words:

. . . THIS NATION UNDER GOD SHALL HAVE A NEW
BIRTH OF FREEDOM. . . .

Committees formed and held meetings. People met and
talked about where they could have the concert.

a momentous an important

had concerns was worried

Examining her heart Carefully thinking about what she should do

Marian looked out on a river of 75,000 people. Her heart beat wildly. Would she be able to **utter one note**?

She took a deep breath and felt **the power of her audience's goodwill surge toward her**. Marian's sisters were there, and Mother, too. Marian stood straight and tall. Then she closed her eyes and sang,

"My country 'tis of thee
Sweet land of liberty . . .
Let freedom ring!"

A roaring cheer followed every song. At the end of the program, the people pleaded for more.

When she began **her thought-provoking encore**,

"Oh, nobody knows the trouble I see
Nobody knows my sorrow.... "

. . . silence settled on the multitudes.

....

utter one note sing

the power of her audience's goodwill surge toward her
better when she saw the audience wanted to hear her sing

her thought-provoking encore the last song that made
everyone think about racism

silence settled on the multitudes everyone became quiet

BEFORE YOU MOVE ON...

1. **Sequence** The manager of Constitution Hall did not let Marian perform because she was African American. What happened after he refused?

2. **Comparisons** How was Marian's life different in Europe than it was in the United States?

LOOK AHEAD Read pages 30–32 to see what Marian does next.

For almost sixteen years after the Lincoln Memorial performance, Marian sang for kings and queens, presidents and prime ministers, famous composers and conductors. She received medals, awards, and honorary degrees for her magnificent voice. But there was still one place Marian had not sung. When she was finally invited, a dream came true.

Marian wondered how people would **react**. No Negro singer had ever done such a thing. She would be the first. But she didn't need to worry. After she signed the contract, someone said, "Welcome home."

On opening night excitement charged the air. As Marian waited in the wings, the orchestra began. **Her stomach fluttered.** She walked onto the grand stage. Trembling, she straightened her costume and waited for the pounding music she knew to be **her cue**.

Tonight was her **debut** with the Metropolitan Opera. **At long last**, she had reached the sun and the moon.

The curtains parted . . .

---

react feel when they saw her

Her stomach fluttered. She felt very nervous.

her cue the sign that she should start singing

debut first time singing

At long last Finally

... and Marian sang.

BEFORE YOU MOVE ON...

1. **Conclusions** Why was Marian's life so important?

2. **Inference** Reread page 30. Why did someone say "Welcome home" to Marian?